ISABELLA DUARTE J.

Poems From My Heart
Words Too Hard To Say Volume II

POESIA PERENNIS EST

⁺°★°ₒ Poems From My Heart °ₒ★°⁺

★·˙˚ Isabella Duarte Jimenez ˚˙·★

Poems From My Heart

Isabella Duarte Jimenez

⁺°★₀° *Poems From My Heart* °₀★°⁺

© 2025 Isabella Duarte Jimenez.
All rights reserved.

No part of this book may be reproduced, stored in a retrieval system, or transmitted in any form or by any means—electronic, mechanical, photocopying, recording, or otherwise—without the prior written permission of the author.

Certain quotes used in this book are drawn from public domain sources, including "Poesia perennis est" (Poetry is eternal).

Some poems in this collection are inspired by existing works. Inspirations are noted where applicable. All rights to the original works remain with their respective owners.

Words Too Hard To Say Volume II

ISBN: 979-8-9991311-0-2

★. · ° *Isabella Duarte Jimenez* ° · .★

To those happy faces,
but sad hearts.
To those distant dreams,
vanished wishes,
and shattered hopes.
To everyone who has been struck
by that small but heavy stone
called reality.

I.D.J.

⁺°★˳° *Poems From My Heart* °˳★°⁺

★. · ° *Isabella Duarte Jimenez* ° · .★

Quick Note

If you were wondering, the flower on the cover is a daffodil. I chose it because, among the many things it symbolizes, the two that speak to me most are **honesty** and **resilience**.

This poetry collection was composed during my seventh-grade year.

With that being said, I hope you enjoy these poems, each one written from the deepest parts of my heart.

⁺°★.° Poems From My Heart °.★°⁺

Cried In The Dark

All those tears were cried
because of how important
that is to me
and it pains me to see
that my dream is so close
to being fulfilled
yet it seems so far away

I know I have to persevere
and I have to keep my head up
I can't lay low
and cry my heart out
I have to go out there
and find a solution

Yet here I am
with a river of tears
and a cloudy sky
over my happy time
I know I shouldn't cry
however, sobbing I am

Here in the dark
weeping all alone
with no idea of what to do
in this vast, cruel world

★. · ° Isabella Duarte Jimenez ° · .★

Fragile Soul

The tears I cried
the feelings I had
the long cold night

I feel numb
and I have no word
My body is shaking
my thoughts are racing

I am grieving inside
with a fake smile
with feelingless eyes
with a fearful heart
and a wordless mind

People's words
come and go
just like arrows
piercing
my fragile soul

Called Reality

Blurry faces
is all I see
There's no one
at arm's reach

Here I am
fantasizing
daydreaming
Thinking of things
that usually never happen

I am picking at my wounds
Unconsciously doing it
until I start to bleed

It looks like I tripped
on a stone called *reality*
It looks like I fell
into a hole called *real life*
It has been happening lately
I'm a little more delusional
than I usually am

Some things that already happened
seem to be happening again
I´ve had that feeling
of delusional hopes
unfulfilled wishes
and shattered dreams

★. · ° *Isabella Duarte Jimenez* ° · .★

That sudden empty feeling
that waits for me
at every corner

I hate not knowing
the reason behind all this
I thought the feeling
was gone
little did I know
it never disappeared

I am exhausted
of tripping over the stone
called *reality*
I wish I could just
never fantasize
never daydream

This shattered heart
can't take any more damage
that my expectations do on me

I wish to be free
to have my peace of mind
to not care anymore
and to stay awake
in reality

Because then
I wouldn't get hurt again

Right?

⁺°★₀° Poems From My Heart °₀★°⁺

Figured Out

Why do I feel
as if I need everything
figured out?
I feel as if I have to know
what I want to do
who I want to be

Somedays
I have my goals clear in mind
other times
everything is blurry to me
I am drowning in a river
of never ending options

And I know I am just starting to live
yet it just feel as if I need
everything to be figured out
if I want to be successful

I have cried multiple times
but no matter how hard I try to find
something that never leaves my mind
I still feel overwhelmed
by all the options that I have

I can be anything
but there is nothing to chose

I could do anything
but there is nothing to do

Isabella Duarte Jimenez

Slow Down

Time ticks so fast
that I don't realize
that it is gone

Seasons change
from night to morning
So fast
rapid going

Please slow down
I'm not living the present
My mind is years away
from where my body is

Time has to
slow down
It has been slipping away
like sand in my hands
An endless flow of water
that will eventually end

Please slow down
give me just a second
to enjoy and appreciate
the life I've been given

Let's just slow down
because soon
I won't be so young

⁺°★₀° Poems From My Heart °₀★°⁺

Time, just slow down
give me just a moment
Can't I look at everything I have
one more time?

My life is a flash
fast like thunder
Things happen so quickly
that it needs to slow down

I have to slow down
I am forcing myself to grow

I have to slow down
soon I'll be on my own

I have to slow down
the world will wait for me

Time
please slow down
give me just a second

For once
let me live in the present
without rushing
without running
without thinking
of what it will be

★. · ° *Isabella Duarte Jimenez* ° · .★

I'm so old now
and the funny thing is
that I don't remember
growing up

Let's just slow down
Give me one night
to thing about my life

(This poem was inspired by the song Slow Down by Laufey)

⁺°★° Poems From My Heart °°★°⁺

Like A Butterfly

Just like a butterfly
I will wait
I will grow
and I'll be free

In the future
I will smile
at my beautiful wings
and fly free

But right now
I'll fight
for my wings
for my life
for my future
for my freedom

I will fly
freely through the skies
and look down
at my old life

Just like the butterfly
I will build my wings
which will help me
reach my dreams

Isabella Duarte Jimenez

Monsters

Our hearts are monsters
wild and carefree
They are foolish
those little blood pumpers

Our ribs are cages
to our reckless hearts
Otherwise
how would we survive?

One Path

Going down one path
because it was the only choice
they gave you

Living a lifestyle
because it was the only way
they told you to live

They told you to follow the crowd
and made an idea of you
in their heads
knowing that you're not
what everyone thinks you are

Different in mind
different in heart
but here I am
where I don't belong

That one path
wasn't meant for me

Reflection

They think I'm different
yet I'm their reflection
I have just mastered
the art of wearing a mask

Is it really
that nobody can see
the real me?

How disappointing
life can be

Third Time

Third time's a charm
but not this time
The luck has somehow
vanished in seconds

Can't figure out why
it just happened like that
I guess *third time's a charm*
isn't so true anymore

★. · ° *Isabella Duarte Jimenez* ° · .★

Not My Own

Crying tears
that taste like the sea
Watching stars
dance around the night sky
Waiting for
the moon to leave
so I can see
the sun once more

In a world where
everything is a choice
it feels like I'm living
a life
that's not my own

Keep Living

The world is spinning
once again
yet my life
still feels the same

Waiting for
my happy ever after
even though
my life has just begun

Thinking that I
might never be happy
even though
I just smiled

Time ticks by
and without a warning
it vanishes away

Yet the world
keeps spinning
and I
keep living

Just like that
I continue
to live my life

★· ·° *Isabella Duarte Jimenez* °· ·★

Selfish

They called me selfish
and said that I
only focus on myself

They said that I
didn't have room in my mind
for anyone
other than me

They said that I
spend my days all alone
and did nothing but things
that do good only to my soul

They said that I didn't care
about any other heart
That I only thought
about my own

They never knew
I did it to help them

They never knew
that their words stung

They didn't realize
that all my hard work
was to help us all
not just myself

Poems From My Heart

Feel Deeply

The waves continue
to play in the sea

The clouds continue
to decorate the sky

The flowers continue
to bloom and grow

My heart continues
to feel so deeply
and with no clue
about the world
it believes that
it will never get hurt

★. · ° *Isabella Duarte Jimenez* ° · .★

Disconnected

Why is it that
I feel so out of place?
It feels as if
there´s nobody else
left for me

It just seems like
I am meant to be
all alone
As if I am a piece
from a different puzzle

And it hurts to see
others laugh and smile
while I am all alone
drowning in solitude

I have cried countless nights
because I felt disconnected
from the crowd

Tell me, am I meant to be
all by myself?
Is there really
nobody else for me?

⁺°★₀° Poems From My Heart °₀★°⁺

I have learned to handle
this feeling of not belonging

Even if it has been
a very long time
why does it still
feel the same?

★. · ° Isabella Duarte Jimenez ° · .★

Words Are Stones

Words are stones
hard and cold
that are thrown
to my fragile soul

They sink in the river
those little stones
making holes
in my broken heart

Yet I don't seem to find
the reason why
these little stones
never bothered me so much

Until now, that is

Keeps Going

Life keeps going
without a stop

I keep living
without a clue

Time keeps ticking
showing me that
my life is passing
before my eyes

I keep growing
not knowing how

I keep smiling
not knowing why

I keep thinking
about all the things
the world has to offer
and of what it will be

★. · ° *Isabella Duarte Jimenez* ° · .★

Wished Upon A Star

One night
I wished upon a star
that all my dreams
will someday come true

The next day
I woke up
with my heart
full of hope

I smiled
thinking that
I could do it

But the clouds
covered my mind

I fell hard
in an abyss called *life*
where the world told me
that I should give up

Then I woke up
from that terrible nightmare
but came to realize
that's how people are
in reality

Afraid Of Forgetting

Afraid of forgetting
the beautiful moment
Afraid that the memory
will fade away

Afraid I'll forget
the happy days
that in the future
won't be thought of anymore

I am afraid that someday
the memory will banish
That those nice little moments
won't matter anymore

But most importantly
I am so afraid
that I won't feel
the happiness
once again

*. · ° *Isabella Duarte Jimenez* ° · .*

Shades of Gray and Black

The solitude
I embraced
and with it
came my happiness
I enjoyed the silent hours
that happened every day

The silence was so much
that the noise of my mind
was tired of not being heard
Then the sea that's in my heart
mad me burst into tears

I cried a river
late at night
that was full of emotions
feelings and memories

The moon came over
shining down at me
and with its moonlight
it wiped my tears

Then the clouds came
dark and gloomy
they covered the moon
and everything above

⁺°★° Poems From My Heart °°★°⁺

I saw various shades
of gray and black
yet with my loving eyes
they weren't as sad
as they actually are

Then I found beauty
late at night

★． · ° *Isabella Duarte Jimenez* ° · ．★

The Trees Danced

The trees danced
showered in moonlight
They swayed
the night away
Rocking to and fro
without a specific direction

They danced so much
that they almost left the ground
just to steal
one kiss from the sky

I do not know
if it was a storm
a blizzard or just
a strong wind
that made the trees dance
to the wind waltz

What a beautiful
thing it was
to watch the trees
dance in the rain
hovered by
the dark
morning sky

⁺°★₀° Poems From My Heart °₀★°⁺

When I Write

When I write
it feels as if
I can finally breathe

As if I found my voice
in a sea of others
As if the clouds
hovering over my head
were cleaned away
to find a beautiful blue sky

When I write
nothing else matters
just my thoughts
just my feelings

It is as if
I go to another world
A world where
I find myself
between words

It is as if my mind and voice
are finally free

★. · ° Isabella Duarte Jimenez ° · .★

Porcelain Heart

The fragile heart
that I hold inside
can carry so much
yet it doesn't break

Not a long time ago
cracks started to from
on my porcelain heart
The feelings that it held
became the tears
that I cried away

Then the fragile heart
that porcelain art
stayed like that
full of cracks

The fragile heart
the porcelain heart
is now broken
shattered on the floor

Free

Writing feels like
breathing the air
that the world
took away from me

Reading feels like
living the dream
that reality
took away from me

Music feels like
hearing soft words
that I could not hear
because people's voices
deafened my ears

For once
it seems that I am free
For once
it seems as if
the world won't
affect me any more

★. · ° Isabella Duarte Jimenez ° · .★

Angel Wings

With those angel wings
that I borrowed from my dreams
I flew so high
that I almost touched the sky

Then reality
and people's voices
took those beautiful wings
away from me

The fall was eternal
a never ending journey
I fell and fell
and couldn't fly
because the angel wings
were no longer mine

⁺°★₀° *Poems From My Heart* °₀★°⁺

After These Years

The memories seem to haunt me
even after all this time
All these years have passed
yet I still cry

I just don't understand
why I still miss them so much
I can't figure out why
but a piece of my heart
was left behind

When I think about it
I want to believe
that it was for the best

And finally
after all these years
I found some words
that express how I feel

Isabella Duarte Jimenez

In My Mind

Sometimes I wonder
if it is all in my mind

Those sad days
and long nights

⁺°★° Poems From My Heart °°★°⁺

Live, Laugh, Love

Live, laugh, love
is an understatement

You have to learn
not just live
You have to experience
sad things too
You have to feel
all the feelings
not just love

Live, laugh, love
or so they say
Life is not painted pink
and it wont give you roses

You also have to cry
you also have to feel lonely
Walk in the rain
with nowhere to go
Walk down the streets
all alone

You have to feel stuck
frustrated, mad
You have to feel as if
every time you walk one step
you walk three more back

★. · ° *Isabella Duarte Jimenez* ° · .★

To be able to live
you have to experience
the things you want to
and the ones you don't

To be able to laugh
you have to know
how it feels to cry

To be able to love
you have to know
the opposite of it
and feel all the feelings
you can possibly feel

Live
such a simple word
that to some people
means something
to others
it means the opposite

Live
something you
cannot do
if out of all the things
I mentioned
you do none

Overthinking

I can't seem to find
a clear voice in my head
where everything
is just a storm
that has lasted days
Where the rain that once
helped flowers grow
is now mercilessly
killing them one by one

With words so harsh
that my own mind tells me
I just lay there
lost in the thoughts
that linger in my mind

The dark skies have arrived
blocking any sunlight from coming
and with that I just seem
to lose myself
every passing second

Trapped in amaze
nowhere to go
Overwhelming things
flooding my head
Something I sometimes enjoyed
seems to kill me
once more

★. · ° *Isabella Duarte Jimenez* ° · .★

Other's Eyes

I think that for once
I'll try to stop seeing myself
through the eyes of people
who never really cared

I guess that now
I will start to see myself
through the eyes of the people
who see me as an angel

Then maybe that way
I'll see myself
through my own eyes
Maybe then
I will see myself
the way I actually am

Time

Time
a constant reminder
that the end is near
yet we waste it all away
when all we do is sleep

We need to wake up
from this nightmare
we call a dream
and just realize
that time is passing by

One day we will see
that all those years went by
and we didn't even care
about the tomorrow
we might not have

★. · ° *Isabella Duarte Jimenez* ° · .★

The Sun Sets

Once again
the sun sets
across the horizon
and just like that
my life will someday
come to an end

Why not shine bright
like the sun
up in the sky?
Why not try
and let everyone
see the light?

One rose grows
small yet beautiful
One day it will have
butterflies all around
the next day
we don't know
what it is all about

The stars in the sky
in a far away distance
today shine bright
but tomorrow
they might be dying

⁺°★₀° *Poems From My Heart* °₀★°⁺

I sit there and wait
for the sun to set
for the time to come
for something to do

Yet as the sun sets
the time passes by
and with no mercy
it will soon force us
to say our last goodbye

★. · ° Isabella Duarte Jimenez ° · .★

Another Life

Perhaps in another life
I would laugh at
what makes me cry
and then maybe
there would be no nightmare
only dreams
that become reality

These past hardships
wouldn't be so sad
Maybe everything
would be just fine

Perhaps in another life
where I see every flower bloom
the sky would be clear
with no clouds around

Then maybe I would go out
more than I usually do
Perhaps I'd laugh and smile
more than I often do

Perhaps I would be happier
perhaps I would be sad
but maybe in another life
I would not think like that

⁺°★₀° *Poems From My Heart* °₀★°⁺

In another life
I wouldn't be like this
In another life
I'd be different
from how
I've always been

In another life
I just wouldn't
be me

★ · ° *Isabella Duarte Jimenez* ° · ★

You Are

You are the words
I desperately looked for
in a sea of letters
in a room full of books

You are the moon
that I needed to shine
over my dark mind

You are the reminder
that one only lives once
That this life
will soon come to an end

You are the only star I see
in a world of galaxies
The flower that I kept
even when I
was offered a whole garden

The thing is
I soon came to realize
that your eyes
and wide smiles
are my own

I soon learned
to be the one
who makes me smile
and laugh, and cry

⁺°★₀° *Poems From My Heart* °₀★°⁺

I finally realized
that I only needed
to find myself
to finally be free

Isabella Duarte Jimenez

Crying Smile

How ironic it is
to smile through my tears
to laugh when I cry
and to say that I'm alright

The water and salt combined
rolled down my cheek
for no reason
for them to be

The eyes watered
yet the mouth smiled
a smile that seemed
to reach the heart

°★° *Poems From My Heart* *°★°*

Three Words

Why should I love thee
when I could have the moon and stars?
Yet thou dost love me
though I've done naught to have that

Three words thou hast spoken
in a million different ways
And thou askest me to speak them too
but I have said them long ago

(Inspired by Shakespeare's **Romeo and Juliet**, Act 2, scene 2, known as The Balcony Scene, from Juliet's point of view.)

★. · ° Isabella Duarte Jimenez ° · .★

Roses Are Red

Roses are red
violets are blue
the world is full of liars
betrayers and more
Yet the roses and violets
keep living with all that
because they have to survive
to bring beauty to this life

We live in a word
where the stars up high
no matter how
bright they shine
they look down to earth
wishing to be
a flower of spring

And the roses look up
to the black night sky
wishing to be
a beautiful star

Roses are red
violets are blue
nobody is satisfied
with the life of their own

⁺°★° Poems From My Heart °°★°⁺

Truth or Dare

Life is a game
of truth or dare

We tell the truth
or slip a lie

We do things
on our own thoughts
or might just
be forced

We all have options
What will you choose?

Truth or dare?
The decision is yours

★. · ° Isabella Duarte Jimenez ° · .★

Goodbye

With sad eyes
and lonely soul
I stepped outside
into the cruel world

With dark skies
full of stars
every memory
seemed to fly

And then it happened
to cross my mind
that very soon
I'll say goodbye

It's Been a While

It's been a long time
since I saw you last
Since the sweet smile
reached my eyes

There's nothing left
for me to say
so I'll whisper a goodbye
and hope for the stars
to someday reply

I'll beg the memories
to stay in my mind
so that way, peacefully
I'll say good night

Those happy days
are long forgotten
We now live years away
from the joy unspoken

★. · ° Isabella Duarte Jimenez ° · .★

Future, Past, Present

The future looks back at me
with those frightening eyes
making me wonder
what path I will walk

The past looks at me
laughing at
the silly little moments
at the mistakes
and regrets

And the present
spontaneous
yet kind
looks at me
with a warm smile
Inviting me
to forget about the past
to not think about the future
and enjoy this simple life

Inviting me
to enjoy the present
because you never know
if tomorrow will come

⁺°★°° Poems From My Heart °°★°⁺

Eclipse

Opposite souls
opposite worlds
One in the night
other in bright skies

Yet they loved each other
so very much
that the clouds and the skies
agreed to let the moon
travel to their world
back and forth

Then the stars realized
that their love was true
and they let the sun
sneak into the night
just so the moon and the sun
could be together

One moment of silence
one of moment of beauty
one moment of darkness
or a moment of light

This little simple luxury
people called an *eclipse*
A small moment
where everything
seems right

★· · ° *Isabella Duarte Jimenez* ° · ·★

Loneliness

A river of loneliness
that's where I am
Where everyone just
leaves me behind

The stars went up
leaving me down here
The leaves fell
and left me looking
at the bare trees

The music stopped
leaving me in silence
The laughs ceased
leaving me
without happiness

Drowning in a river
of solitude itself
but this time it's its twin
called *loneliness*

Sunday Morning

Woke up
to the singing birds
to the melody
of their chirps

The golden rays
fell on my skin
illuminating
the whole room
and the tiny dark places
of my soul

Fresh breeze greeted me
caressing my hair
That Sunday morning
was taken from a movie

★. · ° *Isabella Duarte Jimenez* ° · .★

Tears Fall

My tears fall
for no reason at all
yet I stay like that
without trying
to understand why

The sadness that floods me
wasn't invited into my heart
yet now I lay in bed
with a heart full of grief
while time
just flies away

⁺°★₀° Poems From My Heart °₀★°⁺

Dark Side of the Moon

The moon is beautiful
its silver light shining
yet we all know
there's a part she's hiding

The dark side of the moon
is well kept away
She does not show us
her true self

After all these years
of revolving around earth
the moon still
does not trust anyone
not even the stars

So why should I
expect her to show me
her dark side?

★. · ° *Isabella Duarte Jimenez* ° · .★

Snow

The stars
fell from the sky
and they froze in time
as they slowly fell
on a place called earth

Everyone welcomed
the falling stars
They made earth cold
and the winds strong
They were a perfect excuse
for a movie at home

As the clouds cried
frozen rain
these little stars also slept
while they slowly faded
one by one
covered by clouds
in a gray snowy sky

And these little stars
these frozen drops of rain
were loved so much
that snow they became

As night passed
and snow continued to fall
I came to realize
how beautiful is life

Goodbye II

Singing songs
late at night
Listening to the rain
fall from the skies
Thinking of the people
who said goodbye
and of the people
with who I never socialized

I was hoping for
the tears to fall
For the memories
to vanish
and for them
to stay
But now only
the silence remains

★. · ° Isabella Duarte Jimenez ° · .★

Lost in Thought

A feeling of helplessness
crossed my heart
and tears
formed in my eyes

Draining thoughts
filled my mind
and I started to question
everything about my life

⁺°★°° Poems From My Heart °°★°⁺

I'm Sorry

I want to cry
to scream and die
but I cannot show them
how weak I am
I have to be strong
even through this storm

I'm sorry I'm so weak
I'm sorry I'm a crybaby
I'm sorry it hurts so much
I'm sorry I can't talk

I'm sorry that I
won't take anyone's hand
even if my knees are giving up
and I'm starting to fall

I'm sorry that I
dragged everyone with me
I'm sorry I'm a burden
a very heavy weight

I'm sorry to myself
who's future I perhaps ruined
Who might not be able
to do all the things she wants

★ · ° *Isabella Duarte Jimenez* ° · ★

I'm sorry that I'm sorry
because I shouldn't feel bad
Yet this whole situation
is because of me

I'm sorry I made you worry
I'm sorry I gave you headaches
I'm sorry I refuse help
even when I need it the most

I'm sorry that I
closed all the doors and windows
and drowned myself
in the pain that that felt

I'm sorry I didn't let you in
I'm sorry that I didn't accept help
I'm sorry for wasting the time
I'm sorry for this and that
for everything and anything

No matter how much
I apologize
the weight feels the same
and heavier every second

So I am sorry
very sorry
for being like this
for acting like this
for being sorry
because I shouldn't be

A Kind of Pain

This is a kind of pain
I've never experienced before
A kind of pain
that makes me want to be strong

The tears roll down my cheek
reminding me
that I'm a weak sheep
Making me want
to be in the future
because I don't want to be
in this moment

Perhaps I should go
to before it all began
Perhaps then the pain
wouldn't be here at all

★. · ° Isabella Duarte Jimenez ° · .★

They Figured Out

They figured out
how weak I am
They figured out
that I cry at night

They now know
the griefs of my heart
They now know
how lonely I am

They now think
that I need help
They now think
that I am not okay

It´s a part of me
that I wanted to hide
to leave in the shadows
to deny and deny

But now they have
seen it all
so I guess
I cannot hide
that part of me
that I thought I left behind

Not Like Before

The feeling of being left out
still lingers in my heart
yet somehow it doesn't
feel like it did once

I am left out
wishing I wasn't
but wishing, too
that the feeling
won't be like before

Now it seems
that I've accepted it
It doesn't really bother me
nor it makes me want
to forget the days
when I was never
the one left out

The happiness
is not like before
The rainy days
are not like before
and I still feel
left out like before
but this time
my heart has gotten used to
the loneliness it carries

Isabella Duarte Jimenez

Bittersweet

Winds are stronger
and the rain came back
The clouds move swiftly
and the tree branches dance

Then some accidents
happen to us
and I like to think
that everything
happens for a reason

This bittersweet season
reminds me
I should stay strong
The sour moments
tell me that
complete happiness
is not for us all

We have to keep our head up
because good things come with bad
It all happened for a reason
and it will soon be alright

Summer's Beginning

Everyone told me
that the day felt like
the start of summer
the start of happy days
and warm sun rays
But to me it was only
the end of another chapter
the end of another season
the end of cloudy skies

I saw the warm smiles
drawn over people's hearts
because the sunny days
are almost here

Another summer's beginning
and yet another year

★. · ° *Isabella Duarte Jimenez* ° · .★

Rain

Rain started to fall
like diamonds from the sky
The clouds started to change
to different shades of gray

People started to walk away
knowing that the rain is here
yet I stood still
admiring the beauty of it all

Their Sadness

It all feels unreal
something I never imagined
I really wish
this hadn't happened

No longer worried
about myself
but about
the look on their faces
and the pain
through their eyes

Even if I am the one
with all the agony
their sadness
seems greater than my reality

⋆. · ° Isabella Duarte Jimenez ° · .⋆

The Beauty of a Flower

The beauty of a flower
never really changes
no matter how many storms
it has been through

But the prettiest of them all
can be found
in the most unexpected corners
of this vast world

Home

Home
A word that reminds me
of the old happy days
of the rainy skies
but real smiles

Home
A word that
no longer
has any meaning

When will be the time
that I feel like I belong?
When will I feel
like fitting in
is no longer a problem?

Home
A word I wish
made my heart warm
A word I wish
made me smile
A word I wish
I could understand
or perhaps forget
if it's better like that

Isabella Duarte Jimenez

A Fair Life

They say they wish
life was fair
but if it were
we would all be punished
we would all be betrayed

That is fair
is it not?

Because we all have lied
we've all been rude
arrogant
insolent

We've all been ungrateful
spoiled
selfish

We all have thought of ourselves
as kings or queens
and have overlooked
the people around us

If life were fair
we wouldn't be forgiven
for all the things
we've ever done
said, or thought

⁺°★° Poems From My Heart °★°⁺

But we are forgiven
and we are trusted
We are given
second chances

We are given
more than enough
We are blessed
in ways
we don't understand

So yes
this life isn't fair
because we have more
than we deserve

★. · ° *Isabella Duarte Jimenez* ° · .★

Forgetting

I'm starting to forget
the name of some constellations
and finding them in the sky
has been harder than it once was

I'm starting to forget
all the riddles I knew
all the jokes I told
all the stories I wrote

The memory of
my family's smiles
is slowly but surely
fading away

I can't remember
the lyrics to the songs
I sang with my friends
nor what games
we used to play

Is it normal
to forget such memories?
Should't I
remember it all?

I know I'm not the only one
forgetting the past
but it hurts to know
that the memories won't last

⁺°★°° Poems From My Heart °°★°⁺

Spring

Even if it's still cold
and the sky is barely blue
you know that spring
is about to come
because the trees give
a pink touch to the view

The light became dimmer
as the night came to town
The trees danced
to the windy night

The night was warmer
and there were a few clouds
adorning the sky
That's how you know
that winter will be gone
and spring will come
on its behalf

The sun shines
golden rays on the walls
The skies are blue
like deep ocean azure
The clouds are memories
that float up
into the atmosphere
and birds flew to find
the beauty of something new

⋆. · ° Isabella Duarte Jimenez ° · .⋆

Dulcet memories glide
across the shining sun
and the clouds turned golden
kissed by the sunlight rays

⁺°★₀° Poems From My Heart °₀★°⁺

New Friendships

At last I found
friends of my own
Friends who I can laugh with
and be happy with

They make me feel joyful
as if there's people
who I can trust
They are funny
and laugh at my jokes

They are sweet
fun and kind
I love them
with all my heart
I wish that they too
like me back

These friendships
were serendipitous finds

★. · ° *Isabella Duarte Jimenez* ° · .★

Spring II

Sunny days and clear skies
green grass and dulcet melodies
The flowers are falling
and green leaves are starting to grow
The high temperatures arise
leaving the chilly days behind

The petals are falling
from the trees above my head
They look like snow
those delicate soft cloths
Spring has come
and it will soon leave again
telling us to welcome
the future sunny days

⁺°★₀° Poems From My Heart °₀★°⁺

Moving On

I finally began
to not care about
other people
leaving me behind

I used to see it
as if I couldn't catch up
as if they no longer needed me
and moved on from me

Now I see it
as letting them go
as not caring that
I'll be alone

As letting myself
walk how slow I want
because I do not have to settle
for someone who
will leave me behind

Now I don't walk
at the rear of their back
Now I walk faster
I feel free, and I smile

★. · ° *Isabella Duarte Jimenez* ° · .★

I am now the one in front
and this peace of mind
couldn't compare
to the happiness I felt
when I had what I lost

Voices

The world is quiet
once again
yet my mind is a place
of chaos and fights

I've been hearing voices
from time to time
Voices that sometimes
are hard to understand

Sometimes I
don't speak my mind
because of the fear
of being disliked
A fear that won't go away
chasing me night and day

The voices tell me
I should try harder
I should grow up
and be
what everyone wants

Yet they whisper
their darkest fears
their sorrows and their reasons
to not sleep

⋆. · ° Isabella Duarte Jimenez ° · .⋆

Home II

Let's follow the moon
to get home
and even if we're lost
the stars will guide us

The bluebirds will sing
and help us go far
The sun will show us
the path we'll have to walk

And then
we'll get home
where happiness and warmth
wait for us
and where laughter greets us
with a big hug of love

At last something
among the earth
and the skies above
gives me the joy
I longed a lot before

⁺°★₀° *Poems From My Heart* °₀★°⁺

Leaving Memories Behind

It feels as if
I've left a lot of things behind
but when I look back
all is left is beautiful moments
from the past

The weight of the memories
is slowly sliding off my shoulders
as I leave this place
in which happy moments were made

★. · ° Isabella Duarte Jimenez ° · .★

Silence

Silence
all that I was hoping for
and somehow
it makes me uncomfortable

The wind runs by
whispering things
I'll never understand
Taking away my thoughts
blowing away my feelings
leaving behind
the empty space
that is my mind

The silence now falls upon us
somehow it was surprising
yet it was expected
No words were spoken out loud
all I could hear
was the beat of your heart
and the rising of your chest
every time you take a breath

Misjudged

Misjudged by people's hearts
prejudiced by people's minds
Looked down on by people's eyes
when I just wanted to show them
who I actually am

With judging eyes
they watched me fall
and throwing rocks at me
they expected me to get back up

They left me alone
once in a while
but their thoughts and whispers
flooded my mind

I am being watched
even from afar
They are waiting for the moment
to make me fall
to judge me
and point out my flaws

★. · ° *Isabella Duarte Jimenez* ° · .★

Ethereal Tunes

Beautiful melodies
fly across the room
The rich sound of music
fills my heart with warmth
and it gives me hope
peace, and joy

An ethereal moment
captured in notes
a river of feelings
played in tunes

How can such thing
be so beautiful?
How can such thing
make me smile wide?

It is peacefulness
to which I can fall asleep
It is melodies
that fill my soul with joy

Perhaps it is something
so simple
but to me
it's the whole world

Hail Skies

Gray skies
hover over my head
and hail crystals
fall from above

It is not as cold
as I thought it would be
I guess things can be
different from what they seem

The ground turned white
and the wind blew hard
The storm came by
and rained down on us

No matter how hard
the hail fell
and the wind blew
I just could not stop
being amazed
by the beautiful world
I am in

Isabella Duarte Jimenez

Midnight Storm

The world is quiet
yet once again
my mind starts racing
like a midnight thunderstorm
scary and beautiful

It is a thing to admire
from a distance
because if you get trapped
between thunders and lighting
coming out alive
is not really guaranteed

Do I really feel this way?
Are my emotions an illusion?

The skies are yelling
sending thunder to earth
and at the same time
the flowers bloom
ignoring the storm
they're growing into

⁺°★₀° Poems From My Heart °₀★°⁺

Words To Explain

It seems that I
cannot find the words to explain
the emotions I feel
and the thoughts I think
Although I can write it
all over the paper
I will not be able
to speak such thing out loud

I will forever write
things on paper
even on the walls
as long as I
do not have
to explain myself
out loud
to everyone else

★. · ° *Isabella Duarte Jimenez* ° · .★

Waterfall

The pen slides
swiftly across the paper
while my thoughts and words
flow like a river

It is all a beautiful
waterfall in summer
where my words are the trees
that cover me from judging eyes
and the water is the feelings
that keep me alive

The birds will sing
melodies to warm my heart
and the breeze will whisper
that soon
everything will be fine

⁺°★°° Poems From My Heart °°★°⁺

She Wants To Be

She is quiet
and a ray of sunshine
She works hard
through day and night

She loves to laugh
to talk and smile
She has dreams
that she won´t stop
thinking about
She loves her family
and wishes to be kind

She wants to have friends
but doesn't want to get hurt
She wishes to be
a star in a moonless night
but she is afraid
of people´s judging eyes

She cannot explain
herself to the rest
and would like to sometimes
breathe deep and disappear

She wants to be
enough and the best
but the fear of failure
haunts her happiest dreams

★. · ° *Isabella Duarte Jimenez* ° · .★

She feels as if
she's under pressure
As if comparison
is always around

As if life is a race
a competition to be won
Where the first place
cannot be lost

Remember; Forget

I never really asked myself
if I write so I can remember
or so I can forget

To remember the happy times
the peaceful days
and dulcet nights

To forget the sorrow
the sadness of solitude
the feelings that drowned me
and the questions I never asked

I write to forget
and remember I forgot

I write to remember
that I truly did not forget

To remember and to forget
yet no matter what happens
the memory vanishes
but the feelings remain

★. · ° *Isabella Duarte Jimenez* ° · .★

Privilege

What a privilege it is
to be alive
to breathe in air
and look at the sky
To pick up flowers
from the emerald grass
To smile
and forget about the past

What a privilege it is
to learn and grow
to feel things deeply
and to feel loved
To create things
that amaze the world
and realize that you are strong
even if you are alone

+°★₀° *Poems From My Heart* °₀★°+

Social Anxiety

Shyness eats me up
taking away my voice
It controls my mind
my mouth and my heart

Social anxiety
that is what it was
Awkward smiles
and shy laughs

Scared of messing up
scared of speaking fast
scared of being silly
scared of being seen
as foolish

★. · ° *Isabella Duarte Jimenez* ° · .★

Cherry Blossoms

The cherry blossoms
hold sweet promises
unexpected feelings
and warm times

Cherry blossoms
are like dulcet melodies
Happy memories
that were long left behind

Cherry blossoms
are a reminder
of the feelings I felt
when the petals fell
from the skies above

I know and accept
that I lost things
I wish I didn't know
so I wouldn´t remember

All the memories
are long in the past
and to think of them
is now a waste of time

Nothing can change
or make me forget
the time when cherry blossoms
were a beautiful sight

⁺°★° *Poems From My Heart* °°★°⁺

The petal fell
from the flower I was holding
and the words *I´m sorry*
linger in my head

I believe that it is time
to let go of those moments
yet perhaps I should remember them
everytime a cherry blossom
catches my sight

★ · ° *Isabella Duarte Jimenez* ° · ★

While I Wait for Spring

While I wait for spring
for flowers to bloom
and for sunsets to watch
I sit inside
recollecting past memories
that make me happy
although I cry

While I wait for spring
and for the feelings it brings
my heart longs
for the things that are gone
and the voice in my head
tells me to move on

While I wait for spring
and for new beginnings
for forgetting
and starting over
I just wish
and hope that this time
I will not mind
whatever happens
in this next spring of mine

Forever

Perhaps the meaning
of *forever*
is something
our hearts misunderstood
our souls ignored
and our minds overlooked
As if thinking that
something will last forever
wouldn't harm
our precious smiles

Forever is a word
I think of often
not because
of the word itself
but because of the hopes
that have been broken

The memories still linger
along with my tears
Although soon I'll forget it all
perhaps the feelings won't vanish at all

★. · ° *Isabella Duarte Jimenez* ° · .★

Dandelions

Dandelions are fairies
that hide themselves among the grass
so children can pick them up
make a wish
and blow them away

The wishes made
upon dandelions
will come true
in another lifetime

Blow away
those white tiny fluffs
and watch them fly
to unknown lands

Then perhaps
if you write it on your heart
your wish will come true
and you'll be happy
forevermore

⁺°★₀° *Poems From My Heart* °₀★°⁺

Trees Laugh; Birds Remember

A white butterfly
wanders among the trees
while sunlight shines
on its magnificent wings

The trees start to laugh
their leaves being laughter
while the breeze carries jokes
that it told a thousand years ago

Three ants march by
looking for a purpose
Looking as if they are lost
and waiting for a better future

The clouds are paintings
that were left unfinished
yet they are a beautiful ornament
to the vast blue canvas

Birds tell stories
and respond to each other
about the times when they
were able to touch the sky
Times when they could fly
out of the earth's atmosphere
bathe in galaxies
and dance among stars

★. · ° Isabella Duarte Jimenez ° · .★

The End

It is not the end
not yet
It is just a small pause
a needed break
It is the night
to sleep and recharge
It is that moment
when your mind goes blank

It is not the end
at least not yet
Perhaps it will never be
for with every end
new beginnings come

⁺°★₀° Poems From My Heart °₀★°⁺

Blood of Your Soul

Tears are
the blood of your soul
They are things
your heart wishes to let go

Perhaps that way
the memories will fade
and the sadness and sorrow
will be washed away

★. · ° *Isabella Duarte Jimenez* ° · .★

If I Had Stayed

I wonder how life would be
if I had stayed

If I had said the words
I never spoke

If I had spent time with them
instead of distancing myself
in solitude
between the pages of books

If only I had tried
to make a few memories
knowing that now
I can't see them
anymore

If I had stayed
would I be happy?

If I had stayed
nothing really
would've changed

Detached

I just came to realize
that I'll probably
never belong

Although I am so
close enough to do so
the feelings deep inside me
will bring me back to reality

Feeling detached
falling behind
Laughing
and not know at what
Questions I'll never ask
and conversations I didn't have

It is slowly sinking into me
and although I already knew it
sometimes my heart forgets
but my brain reminds it
that I will never
belong in this place

★. · ° Isabella Duarte Jimenez ° · .★

Bus Ride

The sun rays come
and shine in the window
making everything shine
just like the sky

The leaves on the trees
and the grass beneath
shine like like green gems
that were long lost before

The blue skies above
are softly falling
for no clouds are around
to stop them from dropping

Background music
laughs and voices
and a silent company
of a considered friend

The small feeling
of excitement
of the expected happiness
to soon follow my heart

Solitude

I tend to distance myself
from people
then I ask myself
why I am so lonely
But the trees and breeze
whisper that I'll be fine
and the moon at night
reflects my heart

Perhaps the distance was needed
to mature and bloom
to grow and find
the beauty within solitude

Then I think
that I wouldn't mind
being alone
for a whole life

★. · ° Isabella Duarte Jimenez ° · .★

Clouded Sky

After all these sunny days
and after the bright light
that made my day
the darkness came by
once again

It covered the sky
it took away the light
The birds don't chirp anymore
and the clouds have grown
as if the dullness is back
to blind us all

⁺°★₀° *Poems From My Heart* °₀★°⁺

Time Will Explain

Time will explain
what words couldn't say
what hearts couldn't believe
and what minds couldn't imagine

Time will explain
and things will unfold
so that with your own eyes
you finally see it all

Perhaps regret
will spark in your heart
or happiness will fill
every corner of your mind
Perhaps you wished
you had said the words
but time passed
so it must remain untold

(Inspired by Jane Austen's "Time will explain" quote.)

Isabella Duarte Jimenez

Sweetest Lies

Promises are
the sweetest lies
the mind has known
and the heart has believed

Promises we can't keep
Lies we can't see
Things we thought would happen
and words we thought were said

The slight disappointment
found in time
and moving on
is now not hard

Poems From My Heart

Strangers II

You are now a stranger
who knows my secrets
my sorrows
and my dreams

You listened to all
my important nothings
and one by one
you craved in your heart

We are now just
two strangers
with some memories
With some forgotten words
that were exchanged

Now I only remember
when strangers we were again
and that dream-like memory
I thought I would forget

*(A continuation of "Strangers" from **Poems From My Soul**.)*

. · ° Isabella Duarte Jimenez ° · .

A Year Ago

A year ago
everything was different
and so it will be
a year from now on

That is why it scares me
to think about tomorrow
yet I deeply know that
I should move on from the past

Connecting Dots

I'm connecting dots
that were never meant
to be connected
Dots that were never
really related

I´m making up stories
that seem real in my mind
thinking that perhaps
reality is not
so different from that

Isabella Duarte Jimenez

Trapped

Trapped in memories
trapped in cages
Trapped in words
that were never said

Trapped in those days
when things were different
Looking for a way out
of that bittersweet labyrinth

⁺°★₀° *Poems From My Heart* °₀★°⁺

Loved You Less

If I loved you less
perhaps my feelings would not
be as abundant as my thoughts of you
But my words would flow like a river
for there would be nothing to be ashamed of

All this time has passed
yet I have not uttered the words
I have waited so much to say
Here we are
walking through the gardens
speaking of things
we thought we never would

Although I cannot
make speeches or such
I hope you notice
the meaning of my words

(Inspired by Jane Austen's **Emma**, from Mr. Knightley's point of view.)

★. · ° *Isabella Duarte Jimenez* ° · .★

Just Another

What would be of my life
if I was just another star
in the vast sky?
Just another flower
in a beautiful garden?
And another word
in a long book?
If I was one more
raindrop that fell?

What would be
so special about me
if I was just
another in a million?

Go Back

My mind still
lingers in the past
while the tears I cry
roll down my cheek

Sometimes I wish
I could go back
and enjoy the time
I had
If only I'd known
that I'd miss it all

I guess that
the scars have not healed
and the longing
has not ceased

How I wish
that I could go back
where I belong
and where I found joy

But I guess I will never
return anymore

★. · ° *Isabella Duarte Jimenez* ° · .★

Why Can't We?

Life is too short
to waste it all away
To hide under a rock
and not enjoy the world

Flowers have shorter lives
than we humans do
yet they bring happiness and grace
to every eye that catches their sight

Trees are generous
for they give us oxygen
yet we humans are so greedy
and wish it all for ourselves

Butterflies fly
freely through the skies
showing their wings
unafraid of judgement

Why can't we
do that too?

Not Knowing

Not knowing how to feel
is like not knowing how to bloom
like not knowing how to speak
and not knowing how to grow

Not knowing what to say
is like all freedom and power
is being taken away from us
to leave us vulnerable

Not knowing what to do
is being lost in a maze
with no sense of direction
and not knowing what's next

★. · ° Isabella Duarte Jimenez ° · .★

Every Time

Every time you cry
a star falls from the sky
Every time you laugh
the sun shines brighter
and every time you smile
the flowers seem to sigh

With every breath you take
you seem to wash worries away
and clear the sky
to let the birds fly

⁺°★₀° Poems From My Heart °₀★°⁺

Wishing for a Change

I wish for the world to change
yet I know I will miss
how things currently are

Perhaps I want
to live a different reality
yet recollecting
these past memories
that I have made
will make me wish
to go back in time

I guess that I am afraid
of not liking the change
yet the present is a box
that with each passing day
gets smaller

★. · ° *Isabella Duarte Jimenez* ° · .★

Your Eyes

Your eyes tell a story
that no words could explain
Your eyes are a river
of memories you'll forget

Your eyes are the reflection
of your mind and heart
They tell me
whether you are happy or sad

Your eyes say things
your mouth could not speak
and they are a sea
full of life and wonders

Tears I Cry

The first tear I cry
is a sign of
a thunderstorm to come
It is that drop of poison
that won't let a flower grow
It is that thought
That keeps you from the world

The last tear I cry
is the last cloud on the sky
It is that band-aid
to heal a scar
and that rest
you needed to fly

Isabella Duarte Jimenez

Production of My Mind

They say you cannot cry
without a reason
or so I have been told
many times before

They ask me why
I happen to be sad
They ask me why
the tears began to fall

Can I not be quiet
and lost in my thoughts
for just a second?
Do I have to know
why the salty water
that falls on my checks
is there?
Do I have to have a reason
to be thinking all this?
It is just
production of my mind

Repeating Itself

While looking back
to the long lost past
things flash
right before my eyes
The past seems
to repeat itself
Words are said
once again

Finally knowing
what to expect
what will happen
and what they'll say
Things that already happened
for the first time
seem to be happening
once again

However
I cannot recall
if it is a memory
or a dream

★. · ° *Isabella Duarte Jimenez* ° · .★

Dreamers Often Lie

To sleep is
an opportunity to dream
but if the dream is too sweet
you'll want to say in it forever

It may be so sweet
that it traps you like honey
like words wrapped in velvet
whispered softly in your ear

Reality becomes
nothing but the past
A reflection
you wish not to see
Written words
you wish to erase
but it turns out
that dreamers often lie
and dreams are traps
that hold you tight

*(This poem was inspired by Shakespeare's **Romeo and Juliet**, Act 1, Scene 4, where Mercutio states that "dreamers often lie.")*

Acknowledgements

Words can't express how thankful I am to God, who gave me the gift of writing poetry. He has blessed me and my family more than enough, and I am deeply grateful for everything He has done.

I'm so grateful to mom and dad for all the help and encouragement along the way. Thank you for supporting me in my author journey, for believing in me and helping me reach my goals.

To every reader who found a piece of themselves in these pages: thank you for your time.

Sincerely,

-Isabella Duarte Jimenez ♡

★. · ° Isabella Duarte Jimenez ° · .★

About the Author

Isabella Duarte Jimenez came to the United States from Colombia with her parents and is fluent in both Spanish and English. From a young age, she dreamed of writing and publishing a book, and now that dream has come true.

She loves both literature and music. When she's not writing she will likely be found practicing her violin or cello, at school, reading, or creating art. She enjoys classic literature such as Shakespeare and Jane Austen, matcha lattes, and classical music.

She published her first book at the age of twelve, and this is her second book, released at the age of thirteen.

You can find her Instagram: @isaduj21

.

www.ingramcontent.com/pod-product-compliance
Lightning Source LLC
Chambersburg PA
CBHW031646040426
42453CB00006B/229